Poet Of The Dunes

Songs of the Dunes and the Outer Shore; with others in varying modes and moods

by HARRY KEMP

Provincetown: Cape Cod Pilgrim
Memorial Association: 1988

Vir et Virgo Inter Stellas

Provincetown classics in History, Literature, and Art #1

Copyright 1952 by
Harry Kemp
Reprinted 1988 by the
Cape Cod Pilgrim Memorial Association,
P. O. Box 1125, Provincetown, MA 02657.
Reprinted with permission of Rose M. Tasha,
Literary Executor of the Estate of
Harry Kemp

ISBN # 0-945135-00-9
Library of Congress Catalog Card Number 88-70770

TO HUDSON AND IONE

How beautiful the dawn comes!
The moon is winged with silver,
And brightness kisses every star:
Neither night nor day lack glory
Despite the black disasters of the world
Fallen today on desperate mankind.
Surely the purposes of life are good,
Her long intents, beyond the passing day,—
When she can build such pomp of earth and sky!

Some of these poems have been previously printed in:—Adventure, the Advocate, Ainslie's, The New York American, The Arts Chronicle (London), The New Beacon, Breezy Stories, The Century, The Daily Citizen (London), The Forum, Harper's, Harper's Bazaar, House and Garden, Liberty, McClure's, Munsey's, The Nation, Pegasus, The Saturday Evening Post, The Saturday Review of Literature, The Kansas City Star, Snappy Stories, The New York Times, the New York Sun, Wilshire's, The Bookman, The Old Masses, and The Cleveland Plain Dealer.

POETS OF THE MORNING

Today, of all days,
The world needs poets of the morning
To sing the miracle of the new day
To all the nations; the fresh flower,
The leaf
Edged with the fire of sunrise!—how very few
Behold the dawn I am beholding now!
How many sleep in stale and sated beds
While, swimming like belted Saturn up the clouds
Comes his great, golden majesty, the sun,
To prove the great King Solomon was wrong!

SEA-VISIONS
(On Seeing A Naked Girl Come Out Of The Sea)

I saw a baby merman hushed to rest
By sucking at a mother mermaid's breast;
As I rowed by on a translucent sea,—
Bosoming her babe, she sent eyes up at me.

I saw the bouncing horses Neptune urged
As from the ocean's foam they half-emerged,
And, snorting spume, came rushing at the shore.

I saw these ocean-sights, and many more.

But my last sight was passion's white surprise:
Born out of foam I saw sweet Venus rise!

THE FIRST SONG SPARROW

The year's chill has not yet foregone
Drab evening nor the pallid dawn;
The season is not quite the Spring's
Flower-bright and full of many wings:
But soon the buds will open wide—
The first song-sparrow sings outside.

The bright streak in the crocus soon
Will wake, and wonder take the moon;
The sun will like a strong man come
Martial to an increasing drum:
For there the first song-sparrow sings:
On my roof he folds his wings,
And with bursts of joy he sings!

THE GHOSTLY LOVERS

They seemed to have come from the stars:
    Like voyagers on the moon
Down craters silvery-dusk
    They drifted, dune over dune.
The beach plum blossoms, all-white,
    With never a glimpse of green,
Like little ghosts in the dark
    Beleaguered the moon-washed scene.
We stepped back, letting them pass,
    Lest, immaterial, they
Might sense our bulkier world
    Blacken across their way . . .
The foam fled, white, on the beach,
    Spreading phantasmal pearl
As the ghost of a man went by
    Wooing the ghost of a girl.

HOW THE COLOR OF GREEN CAME
INTO THE WORLD

(Written the night I saw a green moon)

The Third Day of Creation had begun:
The Lord God asked the Angel of the Sun
(This was the day when trees and grass were made,)
"What Color shall we give the trees that shade
"The ground with grace?—the leaves of tender grass?"
The Archangel of the Sun, brought to this pass,
(Uriel his name,) said, "Let me think a while;
"For miracles must have their proper style!"
Then, after pondering deep, "There's your great moon,
"Jehovah, standing at its plenilune:
"Lend me its broad face for experiment!"
Then Uriel seized a comet where it bent,
And made its tail a brush, dipped it in gold
Of sunset; took the last blue of the sky,
With a great, sweeping stroke, precise and bold
Of cometary brush, to set thereby,—
Yes, with the full moon's face for a palette,
He mixed two colors till one color met
Upon its face, by all the angels seen:
It was the color Adam named as **green;**
Good, restful **green,** that, since, fills all men's eyes
With quiet joy, with somewhat of surprise
Forever: such the Power and Dream God gave
To men, who need not be the Seasons' slave:—
With promise, if they're innocent and wise,
Of the **eternal green** of Paradise!

MOON-MAGIC

Three silver birches wait outside my door
All-lovely in the silent evening air
That sunset and its following star makes fair:
Yet something still they seem to tarry for
In this strange hush expectant everywhere
Of some new foot of wonder on night's stair,
Something till now the lords of dusk forebore,—
As if, once lent, no beauty could be more!
Three haunted, slender birches wait outside
My door, and shadowy-lovely are the three,
And lovelier still the first, great stars that shine:
Then—in the birches stands the moon, and she,
The amorous Eve's enchanted, silver bride,
Takes night with single wonder and divine!

SUMMER'S HERE AGAIN

Tell all the world that Summer's here again
    With song and joy; tell them, that they may know
How, on the hillsides, in the shining fields
    New clumps of violets and daisies grow.

Tell all the world that Summer's here again
    That white clouds voyage through a sky so still
With blue tranquility, it seems to hang,
    One windless tapestry, from hill to hill.

Tell all the world that Summer's here again:
    Folk go about so solemnly and slow
Walking each one his grooved and ordered way—
    I fear that, otherwise, they will not know!

NO CAUTIOUS CHARTS

The Captain who puts boldly out to sea
And does not skirt the cowardly coast, has led
Ever, Man's long advance: speak not to me
Of cautious charts and old men's proverbs said
To drag against the soaring ecstacy.
Without God's fools where would the Present be?—
Bridegrooms who took Disaster to their bed
And gave the world a golden progeny.
To woo Destruction with so fair a face
Is better than to rot in one sure place:
Sometimes a Cause is nothing till it's lost.
For all this soon-dreamed, passing life of ours
And fear of thorns that guard consummate flowers,
Give me the man who does not count the cost!

VACATION

Wiping the dust of the City off,
Does one need to be reconciled
To a vast, immaculate beach,
And to a sunset the last beauty of the world
Followed upon by a silver-shadowed moon?

GULLS DURING VERY SEVERE STORMS

I wondered where the gulls went during storms
Too great to lift through like blown paper forms.
I heard the exploding surf assault the strand.
What blanket of gray stirred over this dark sand
That dipped to the kind shelter of the land?
The sudden sun, like a light-stricken moon,
Swam rapidly forth, to disappear as soon.
It was then I came upon the gulls that stood
Thick as abundant branches in a wood,
Waiting the wind's fall. Of their multitude
Not one rose up, with wavering drifts to follow
From the safe shelter of the dune's dark hollow.
They feared the storm more than my near surprise.
A stir went through them, but they did not rise!

A CAPE COD STORM

The gulls lift, balanced high, on riding wings
Not only my rhyme, my lifted spirit sings!
Shielded from strident sand, my eyeballs reach
Across the seething, furious, blanched dominion
Of waves and foam and breakers bellowing in;
Where the sea's lips of fury flange out, thin,
One shore-bird scutters with a broken pinion,
Astonished, here and there, about the beach . . .
The purple-brackish sky's all-written by
The pallid-branching lightnings, as they ply
Celestial script of their robust delight! . . .
I wish that God had never let me write
Because there's music here and music there
And my small pen cannot transcribe the air! . . .
I seek the song I've never overtaken;
I face the power I cannot re-awaken
In words; though, this wild day, the storm has given
The beauty of all music, lightning-riven;
That struggling fisherboat perceives the glory—
Yet I stand here, and cannot tell the story . . .
It is a song that only you can sing,
O, Storm!—that, like the heightening play of life,
No poet ever yet has put in Song:—
I lift my prayer up to the gods of strife,
To strike against my sleep their pulsing gong!

A SUNSET FIT FOR ANGELS

A sunset fit for angels took the sky,
It swam in archipelagoes of light.
The silent music of the stars of night
Followed on sunset's crimson harmony
That, fading, brightened still in memory
As eagles climb to nests of high delight
Where, great above the world, the tops stand, bright,
While, far out, washing outward, looms the sea.

Next door to life was heaven: all the world's woe
Somehow seemed part of false disaster's dreams
That haunt the sleep-bound spirit till it wakes . . .
I trust that what that waking is, I know:
The sun that sends its backward, waning gleams,
Forward into a bright, new morning breaks!

THE SHIPWRECK

Men stood like dolls about the seething deck;
White as the foam their faces shone, whose fleck
Tongued far up the long slope, where in the sky,
Other men huddled but to watch men die.
In vain they sent the line. No boat could ride
Upon the back of that tremendous tide.
The fire they lit, the great wind blew it out.
Fallen to a whisper seemed each urgent shout,
Cupped hand to ear. The watchers waited there
Lashed by the sand as if whips filled the air . . .
The ship was borne asunder by no shock
Riven, and dangling piecemeal on a rock,—
It was no reef it struck on, utterly breaking
Asunder into jutting beams, and taking
The foamy coil and wash of lifted seas:
Its seamen knew some moments of false ease
As on the long, low hidden bar it ground,
Shaken from end to end, yet every timber sound:
But then the seas, the trampling seas, began
As in one grey, concerted giants' plan,
And over and over, and over and over they bore
While Help irked, helpless, half a league from shore . . .
And when with dusk the great wind ceased to blow,
Men caught them where the long surf brought them in;
Men drew them up beyond the coil and din;
Men battled for them with the undertow;
Men laid them out like stiff dolls in a row.

A SATISFACTORY LIFE

The sun, the wind, the moon; stars, birds, beasts about me:
O, this is the kind of life I want forever:
Thought by geographies; all details of pettiness
Erased by bright dune-days,—
Days of good, new dawns; never-forgotten sunsets;
Nights when the sky is high as God with stars;
Times of the halcyon on brooding seas
Where joyous porpoises roll and prank like clowns.
My shack standing in the middle
Of all this, in the midmost
Of the leagues of sand, of the long, rolling leagues,
Next door to heaven and close on the gates of sunset,
The opening doors of dawn:
I've got what few have, I've got the life I want!

MUTUAL POSSESSION

O, you've got me, and I've got you:
  It is a bargain love has made,
Which, if we gave no answer to,
  Our lives themselves would stand betrayed.

As if no other can be known
  Let us enjoy this day begun:
The trumpets of the dawn have blown;
  Now blooms the rose, now shines the sun.

Yesterday's kisses have not been;
  Tomorrow is the world's deceit,
False realms for ghosts to wander in,—
  Both past and future are a cheat:

For yesterday has flown away;
  Toomorrow leads with phantom drums—
Because there is no yesterday,
  Because tomorrow never comes.

Here stands my shack upon the shore;
  There moves the vast, eternal sea:
Than this day let us ask no more
  Since I have you, since you have me!

TITANS' LAND

Here is the place the Titans might have striven,
Here where these barren slopes of sand produce
Beauty no human cunning puts to use:
The land is scarred, the land is cleft and riven
By edging tide and ever-biting wind;
Defiant-topped, the stalwart tree-van, thinned
To scantest growth, fights to victorious loss;
Half-stripped of green the bone-bare branches toss.

This mighty end holds room for no small feeling,
This end of ocean-sky-encircled land
Held fast with veritable ropes of sand
Where now the sand, and now the waves, come stealing
In ambush on each other, and where blend
The land and sea in war that knows no end.

And where at night the Northern Lights disperse
Long, ghostly shafts that search the universe!
Thus kept in awe, in bounded power of light
Remain the ordered phalanxes of night.

The Titans, glorious in their whelmed endeavor,
Have struck the Gods back to their lazy bounds
And mean, monotonous, victorious rounds:

The Gods!—their life is incense mortals raise!—
The stricken Titans scorn both prayer and praise!

CAPE-RETURN

To make me feel like one that walks
    On the body of the moon,
There will be a craterlike, silver sweep
    Of dune over shadowy dune.
I will climb up into a zigzag sky
    Through sand like snow in a dream:
To lighten their burden I will trudge
    Behind the struggling team.
My shadow, as I follow them,
    Will reach out, long, behind,
To cling against my wading feet
    Like one led, being blind.
All other life will loom, foregone,
    But a clump of surprised, low pine
Lost in a hollow's scattered green
    By the long, lapsed sea-line:
And I'll hail their richness of paucity
    Where nature reveals no more
Than the sand of a coast that is distance-lost
    On an ever-rustling shore.

INDECISIVE DAY

The morning didn't know what it wanted to do
From the first upward clamour of the sun
Striking the under-sides of somber clouds
To feathery, interlaced vermillion.
Over the tawny tops and slopes of the dunes
Racing madly the stormy sunshine blew.
The morning didn't know what it wanted to do,
So it climbed into indecisive day.
Wind rose, and rain. The architecture fell
Of proud-housed clouds: the eye caught chasms of blue
Soon over-swept by veils of diamond-grain.
At times a spectral, daytime moon waned through,
And then the windy sun spun forth again.
Gulls tossed high through the indecisive day
When morning didn't know what it wanted to do.
There marched a silvery fog that bivouacked through
The purple hollows, in scattered groups like men—
While somewhere a voice like a dream was heard to sing
How indecision can be a lovely thing!

FISHER-TOWN

Their life's the sea's. By following any street
Your feet will find the waves at either end.
Old fishnets serve for fences. The land is shaken
Like a ship's deck by all the storms that waken,
Darkening from sky to sky. There's a calm seat
Where captains sit who sail the sea no more—
Aged, but hale and oaken to the core,
To whom the ocean was a trusted friend.
About the long-wharved, huddled fisher-town
Men's talk assumes the ocean's undertone;
Their motions go like gradual nets let down,
And each man stands as on a deck alone.
Even when they group in waiting idleness
The sea's tang stays about them ;they confess
In every mood they are the ocean's own.
Their girls who tread the street go trim and neat
Like ships whose sails and pennants gleam, complete;
Their wives, too, serve the sea who stay at home
While their men's dancing vessels urge the foam.
The very earth's a ship, and they, its crew—
Their life's the sea's; sometimes their death is, too!

THE FOG

The fog sweeps up, a chaos of marching White
As visible as day yet blank as night,
Pouring and tumbling in and surging about.
A phantom army whose advance is rout,
Whose battle-line, oblivion everywhere;
Leagued with the onward motions of the air
Begot of space conjoined with emptiness.
The foghorns call like prophets in distress
Over disasters life has not yet known.
A bell subtends its dim, lost monotone.
One after one, the houses blot from sight,
One after one, sunk deeper than in night,
Each landmark stops existence, and, unseen,
Objects drop out, with a white night between . . .

One strayed existence, and but one, abides:
Above the invisible rippling of the tides
A solitary, grey gull sifts its way
Wing-faltering down a vastitude of gray,
A soul that seeks a drowned, familiar shore
And screams because its world exists no more!

The fog retreats, recoiling from the wind;
In rolling banks it breaks back, fuming thinned:
Slowly the invisible earth returns, here, there,
A dune, a street, a house; the open air
Falls free in straits and vistas, and the mist
Lies caped and islanded; last, blue, a-twist,
Like lazy household smoke it mounts in space
And gives the world back to its wonted place.

THE MORNING AFTER

My shoes stood pointing forth as if
  They wanted to go far away;
My coat clung, rowdy, to a chair;
    Where they'd been dropped, my trousers lay;
   I glimpsed my freshly laundered shirt
   Wooing the hearthstone's unswept dirt.

My necktie draped the electric light;
My socks were birds that fell in flight:
All my habiliments pointed out
The fact, beyond a sober doubt,
Their master came home drunk, last night!

WORLD OF CHANGE

In a world of illusion and change
Where the faithfullest friends grow strange,
Where values shift over-night
And dule takes the place of delight,—
I know it is folly to ask
Of Love, fearing shoulders to task
For danger of crumpling a wing,—
A serious face for this thing:
Yet I'd like, for a little while,
To reign as the only one:
So give me a kiss with a smile,
And let's be true, just for fun!

I WANT TO KNOW ABOUT YOU

I want to know about you:
What you did yesterday;
What happened to you lately;
What you expect tomorrow:
I want to hear about you—
The news of your whole being!

STRANGE ACQUAINTANCE

Each looks in the other's face
    As he passes to and fro,
Forgetful of the fact that he greets
    A being he does not know:
While trivial, dying things
    Are smiled at, and discussed
With a spirit clothed in mystery
    Who inhabits a house of dust!

CARELESS PILGRIM

Though I've always counted my losses
    Small, in return for a song,
I have been a careless pilgrim
    Friends have protested, too long!
Yet if the procession passed me
    While I stopped for a flower,
I've found rich gifts by the wayside
    That rewarded the vagrant hour:
Lagging the critical moment
    Where the light's spear is thrust,
I chanced on miraculous roses
    Sprung from incredible dust!

SOMETHING THEY'VE MISSED

There must be something they've missed
    That the sages lack wisdom to tell,
If the turn of a woman's wrist
    Can lead men to heaven or hell;
If the taste in a cup of wine
    Can change the face of the day,
Or one rose make a whole bush divine,—
    Then life must be wiser than they:
They thrust me forth from their school;
    I joined the crowds in the street:
I found all the world was a fool—
    But the folly of life was sweet!

NAUFRAGIUM

Though I'm a broken wreck in wave-washed sand,
Do, Poet, sing the song that truth must say:
Call no one's pity on me any day,
For I've been everything the builders planned.
Don't hawk a threnody about the land
On me; I have borne up the glittering bay,
Glittering more brave, myself; treading the spray,—
No other ship has been more great and grand.

Though full of shells and sand and long-topped weed,
Is it not something to have been? to have gone
Vast voyages where alien stars abide,
Shaking whole oceans from each streaming side,
With satisfaction in the accomplished deed?—
All I have been is mine. I envy none.

THE OLD SHOEMAKER

The Old Shoemaker is gone.
The days of sound and single craftsmanship
Close with him, when men once knew all a trade,
Not parts and snippets of it, piecemeal doled
From ranged assembly lines, levers and treads,
And not a man's intelligent, full work.
The shoes he made were good shoes made entire
By hand and awl and thread plied diligent.
He had canaries in cages for companionship.
His canaries that sang and bred in cages hung
About the room, are sold.
His shop is dismantled.
The old wood-stove like a grieved thing stands all cold.
In that quaint, one-roomed shop
Friends sat talking sparely; he would put in
A word of wisdom now and then, sure, practiced
As his stitching, his quick hammer.
His was a voyaging mind, a pilot's thought
And quenchless fire of an undaunted heart.
The Old Shoemaker is gone.

WIND OF CHANGE

There was a wind rose over-night:
Each wave became a burnished height,
Then fell to silver when it broke
In tufts of laps lazuli smoke.
The tasselled dune-grass blew oblique;
Upon the dunes' remotest peak
I saw the bright sands scurry and run
Like lively small folk in the sun
Lifting a diamond here and yon.
My shack that holds my books and me
Grew like a ship that walks the sea;
I quite forgot I had been born
Before that bright, tumultuous morn:
I put all other days behind
For that bright day of voyaging wind!!

SHIP-GLAMOR

When there wakes any wind to shake this place
This wave-hemmed atom of land on which I dwell,
My fancy conquers time, condition, space,—
A trivial sound begets a miracle!
Last night there walked a wind, and, through a chink,
It made one pan upon another clink
Where each hung close together on a nail—
Then Fantasy put forth her fullest sail,
A dawn that never dies came back to me:
I heard two ships' bells echoing far at sea!
As perfect as a poet dreams a star,
It was a full-rigged ship bore down the wind,
Piled upward with white-crowding spar on spar;
The wonder of it never leaves my mind.
We passed her moving proudly far at sea:
Night was not quite yet done, nor day begun:
She stood, a phantom of sheer loveliness
Against the first flush of an ocean dawn:
Then, at the elevation of the sun,
Her ship's bell faintly sounded the event,
While ours with a responding tinkle went . . .
The beauty life evokes, outlasting men,
It fills my world from sea to sky again;
It opens on me like a shining scroll—
The Ghost of God that ever haunts the Soul!

THE POETS

These are the ones who dared to dream, despite
The purblind fools who strove to set them right;
These are the ones who dared to dream in vain
When judged by yardsticks of the merchant's gain:
Because **their** vision pierced the universe,
And counted stars like silver in a purse,
And found the sun life-giving, manifold
In riches past the power of hoarded gold.
Where ancient bigotries the lie proclaimed
These took a pagan mistress unashamed;
Where Science set up bigotry's new rule
And blank mechanics of a barren school
To govern souls,—these Singers did not yield:
Song was their Sword, and Song, their Battle-Shield:
Above the pitiful, blind, stumbling throng
They walked, companioned by the Lords of Song!

TRANSIT GLORIA

Our sun, with all its worlds, drops down the sky,
For, banked in shining heaps, the great suns fly
Onward in fiery swarms like golden bees,
While from all sides the everlasting seas
Of night break on them as they thunder by . . .
And ignorant generations live and die
Amid this storm of stars, and feel at ease.

GREAT NIGHT AND CRICKET'S SONG

While in my hut brisk, hidden crickets sing
The dusk leads on night's world on world of stars;
Except where in the East two fading bars
Spy down on where the sun went, everything
Strikes beyond human reach; infinity's wing
Brushes my troubled thought; red-throbbing Mars
Broods yon; and yon Aldebaran's alien wars
Perturb my heart to strange imagining.
Caught in the compass of a minim being,
A thing of earth while all space takes my seeing,
Stretched on the rack of infinite time and space—
What is it lifts my blood's small, inner pace
To this unutterable evening's prime:
While with my pulse the crickets' song keeps time!

CAPE'S END

There is battle here, there is clean and vigorous war,
There are bivouacs visited by night's every star,
There are long, barren slopes of enchantment burned clean by
    the sun
And ramparts of strange, new dreams to be stormed and won.
Here the five-petaled wild-rose blossoms more sweet
Because the earth is barren and the heat
Intolerable for lush, domestic grass;
The ocean shines like many discs of brass,
Or between white hollows it lapses, great and green,
Where solitude sifts slowly in between
The hills of sparkling waste that rise and fall—
Hills whose one music is the seabird's call . . .
And here is all space that ever eye can see:
The ocean, completing all immensity,
And the sky, mother of infinity;
Where greatness on smallness jostles till both are one
And a grain of sand stands doorkeeper to the sun!

OCEAN SAND

Pushed back, it pours forth again,
Unnumbered, indisciplined sand:
Its nature's to gain on the land,
A threat to the order of men.
In billions it paces the beach;
It climbs, caught about by sparse green;
Nothing can make it unclean.
The clouds wander over, the sky
Leans blue as a harebell, nearby.
Here ships come, easy, to shore,
Caught over the bars' sunken breast;
Slow seas, smoking aft and to fore,
Bring a dirge for an aeon of rest:
Such ships will run no more for gold;
The rich sands will crowd up each hold;
Their figureheads soon will be quelled;
Their names soon forever witheld.
For here, where the warm, random cup
Of a girl's hand can gather it up,
Sand cares for no fame but to be
Infinite granite worn down
From cliffs where eternity
Sat, young, before Time got renown!

EXPLORER'S HEART

The trees rose tier on tier; and shelf on shelf
Of climbing green massed branch on thwarting branch
Till he fell back in panic on himself;
Briars broke against him in their rough array
And fetched red streaks across him which to staunch,
Panting he stopped, in a chance rift of day . . .
But now the brush gave way to barren land
And he struck on fresh prints which brightened hope
That some one recently had passed that way:
Then he recalled this was the very sand
Where he had first diverged down the great slope;
And after hours of error he'd got back
To the same place where he at first grew lost:
His heart sang, as he found, by his own track
The homeward trail and good familiar coast . . .

The Moral will not please home-keeping wit:
That trail must haunt him till he conquers it.

PURITY

Be pure, sweetheart, but not like snow
Which soon its whiteness must forego:
Be fierce and pure as fire may be
Which burns away impurity.

TWINS OF FLESH

Love without lust
Is tasteless as dust;
Lust without love
Is a swineherd's drove.

QUICKSANDS

The land had end before the sea began
And fell halfway between the shore and sea:
As if creation halted in its plan
Overawed by its task's immensity,
Bestowing less than chaos with a hand
Too opulent in width of sea and land—
The shore had end before the sea began . . .
And neither boat went there; nor any man,
Nor any creature ventured perilously
On that grey space that was nor land nor sea . . .
For its grey wastes went down beneath the weight
Of the least shell that left no imprint there,
And the swift shore-bird sought escape too late
If it but hesitated in the air.

THE GULL'S STAUNCH VOICE

Here in this ocean-haunted solitude
The sea-gull is my very bird of song:
True as at sea the ship's hour-telling gong,
His voice fits with the tenor of my mood.
I never feared that Right would yield to Wrong,
In my young thought; and less I fear today
When many mouths of ill walk, false, abroad:
Still sure horizons wait the sun's good way;
And still the bright, green life lifts from the sod.

That's a far cry from sea-gulls?--Not at all!
The gull's voice lifts me like a trumpet-call.
That resolute bird my bent of soul has made:
I've heard him calling through the great, slow mist;
He sends a steadfast voice, nor is afraid
That fogs will make the world cease to exist.

TERMAGANT'S RETURN

When you bring back, after a little while,
The merciless, bland sweetness of your eyes,
The slow electrocution of your smile—
My friends will pity me, my friends will say
"When once she left, she should have stayed away!"
They'll think you've but come back to wear me down,
Making of me your tortured lout and clown!
But how you nag my slackness into life
And damn and goad my being into bliss
Till hell's self gives red gates on paradise,
How you show whole worlds from a precipice
Of hate, that, strangely wedded to delight,
Makes Love and Rancour an hermaphrodite—
What friend is wise enough to fathom this?
Our life's no snail that finds each inch a mile;
Black, utter boredom, the world's malady,
Weighs never, I can swear, on you and me!—
My life's necessity, my soul's despair!
Renew what inward honor must deplore;
Restore our pristine heaven of disgrace! . . .
Some day six cops will march in at my place,
Having with their shoulders broken down my door—
To find your silenced body on the floor,
And me, heart-broken, waiting for the Chair!

ULTIMATE CHALLENGE

Especially if their lading be a dream
Ships must go lonely if they'd voyage far;
Feeling the upsurge, through each brace and beam,
Of fuming oceans; top to shrouded spar
Set to the following of a single star!—
There's no safe compass, where the hidden gleam
Sits behind clouds, and when blind tempests stream,
Except the guiding laurels faith would wear!

There often bide black gales and bursting beams,
And sails that fly in rags from broken spars:
There are no charts for ships that follow dreams
And crowd up sails against the beckoning stars:
Don't sign aboard—unless you're certain you
Can dare a wreck, and deem it glory, too!

SUBMARINE PRACTICE-RUN

Beyond the shallows where the last buoy floats,
Beyond the nets, beyond the fisher-boats,
Leviathan rejoicing in the sun,
The submarine swept on its practice-run
Where it wooed blank submergence and the blind
Descent whose courage kept the ocean kind!—
Onward a space the trailing periscope shone;
Then it deceived the eye, too, and was gone:
Where it had been, a wave ran; and, beneath,
Moved men who dared the greedy throat of death ..

Black-dotted strollers went along the sand
And gazed out where the many-moving, bland
Crests tumbled.

A lone whale that lazed up spray
Seemed to assist the boat upon its way.

THE WORLD'S BEAST
(From Heine)

It is the Wood of Old Romance;
   The linden's bloom hangs sweet;
The white enchantment of the moon
   Takes every sense complete.
I have no sooner stepped inside
   Than up the great sky goes
A thrilling voice—the Nightingale's!
   She sings love and love's woes:
She sings of love and lovers' woes,
   She sings of tears and laughter;
Her joys are so sad, her moans are so glad,—
   Forgotten dreams wake after.
With but a further step I find,
   Climbing the moon's broad face,
A tower-topped castle, all one hush,
   Set in a mighty space.
Behind each gloom-carved window barred
   Such brooding sadness lies,
No doubt the very Body of Death
   Waits God there with closed eyes.
Before the castle's silent door
   There squats a dreaded thing
With half-shut eyes the more alert,
   Strong bulk that needs no wing!—
Man-womanish, monstrous frightfulness,
   Lusts centuries-bequeathed,
A woman's face, breasts bursting high,
   Beast-bodied, claws half-sheathed . . .
O, Christ! but she was beautiful
   With that white light on her face,
With that little smile of haunting lusts
   No slyness could erase!
What mortal man could stand and look
   Unmaddened by that sight?—
And, O, but the nightingale sang sweet
   And, O, but the moon was bright! . . .

I took the step that I must take
  Though it drew down my doom;
Aching, I kissed the sullen lips
  While Paradise burst in bloom;
Aching, I met those great, bland eyes,
  And the honeyed torment grew;
Hell also brought fierce, little flowers
  Fed with men's veins like dew.
The great arms rose and caught me close,
  The great, unsheathed claws tore;
While the strange, fierce kisses increased the ache
  The laugh grew to a roar.
My soul was sucked up from my heart
  So mad-sweet was the pain
As I mated the World's Beast kiss for kiss
  While I bled from each little vein.
And the Nightingale sang, "O, lovely Sphinx,
  "O, Love, life's hope and woe,
"Say, what is this thing of Hell's last pang
  "And the last bliss angels know?
"For thousands of years I have poured my song
  "While the stars fled, spark on spark,
"Hoping at last you would speak the Word,—
  "And I still sing on, in the Dark!" . . .
The Castle underneath the moon
  Stood high, like a dreaming hill;
The Body of Death that slept inside
  Stirred once, and then lay still!

NEW ENGLAND CHARACTER

New England character is so deep-hidden
That more than once I've said, of these fine people:
"Their passion held tight-lipped, their few words spoken
"Stem an unspoken torrent not let go."
I sometimes think the curb that's in their blood
Hides too much strength, not spareness, too great seed
To break into abundance; as their stony
Hillsides grow Sweet-Juicy-Pears that melt
To prized, immediate sugar in the mouth,
Blackberries yielding easily to the touch,
Big huckleberries lush on little trees!
O, their luxuriousness of summer weather
That we come to enjoy, should undeceive us,
Their ready help that makes no protestation,
To any, even a stranger, who's in need;
Their speechless, awkward Christian aid of neighbours
Which needs no lesson from the Good Samaritan! . . .
Only they don't leave diaries of their lives
Before each curious-minded boarder's gaze!

BAYBERRY FANTASY

I wondered why they faintly seemed to glow
Though the sun had departed hours ago:
Was it because they remembered earlier days
When half of life was work and half God's praise
And ghostly bayberry bushes greyish-white
That glimmered gently under stars at night
Afforded taper candles prim with beauty
To help the Puritan wife's domestic duty!

THE SINGER PASSES BY

A Singer goes along the streets
  With a sweet and burning song
Of "love me just a little bit
  "If you can't love me long!"
Though he loathes a kiss that ends too soon,
  He knows that all things range
Where love is subject to the Moon
  And life's a slave to change.
He knows that Beauty's feet are led
  By Time's impetuous drums;
That soon today is yesterday,
  And tomorrow never comes.
His song lifts at each window's blank,
  And those who live inside
They hear that Love is passing by,
  And fling their windows wide.
The people look, and find him gone;
  They look upon the sky;
They turn to kiss the one they love—
  But the Singer has passed by!

FAILURE

I watched a sail upon the restless sea;
  It came and went beneath a cloud-vexed sun:
So, all through life, like glimpses come to me
  Of things that men have sought and have not won:

But there's more happiness in the Unfulfilled
  Often, and in the Imminent Might-Have-Been;
And Wonder leads the faltering hand, self-willed,
  That takes the Splendid Chance, and fails to win!

TOGETHER

Then set the furniture about the room,
And cut the flowers, soon deprived of bloom,
To wait in vases; and have the table-ware
Polished and bright, to grace the daily fare.

It must be daily, yet as days must be,
Parcelled and portioned of eternity.
Summon your braveries; for here is need
For courage for the bright, recurrent deed!
If we break the virile bread, pour the soft wine
Without the daily sacramental sign,
Proffering false idolatries instead—
Flat will the wine fall, stale will grow the bread.
Still full of starry courage this must be,
This luminous circle gathering you and me,
This great adventure cased in blood and bone
And pulsing flesh, companioned yet alone!

CHAUCER

He went abroad in England's greenest May;
He gathered earliest hawthorne from the bough.
And rode to quaint shrines where with simple vow
Plain speech came clad in honest white's array
And what men had to say men needs must say:
Words too-nice ears to-day might not allow:

Though in the Bible God did such I trow
Whose kings upon their knees feared not to pray.

And Chaucer still goes singing down the years
With speech out-moded and with meaning quaint;
While not till Maytime's blossoms come no more
And dew no more upon the rose appears
And earth's last blossom takes Time's cancered taint
Will his bright pageants reach the last dim shore!

ALL I CAN GIVE

All I can give is a song,
    And that is best,
Which down the ages will prolong
    Our names, when all the rest,
The good, the bad, the glad, the brave
Become lost headstones on a grave:
    If poets are a little mad
    Their singing makes the whole world glad!

THE HUMMING BIRD

The sunlight speaks and its voice is a bird:
It glimmers half-guessed, half-seen, half-heard,
Above the flowerbed, over the lawn . . .
A flashing dip, and it is gone
And all it lends to the eye is this—
A sunbeam giving the air a kiss.

THE MADMAN

I had a vision in the night:
That vast, mysterious something,
That which hangs imminent in orchestras,
That thing which every human heart expects,
I dreamed had come to me;
Sometimes I felt it hanging over me
Like the shadow
Of enormous catastrophe,
And then again it was the liberation
From everything,
The unpremeditated event
That hovers, infinite, over every man . . .

No, it is not death,
Nor love,
Nor fame, success; nor wealth:
These are but paltry things,
The sparrow's wing before the archangel's flight . . .

Day after day I felt that it would happen
Of which all mankind feel the imminence
As Christians dream a great, red Judgement Day
And dip their lives into its dreadful color . . .

And now it must have happened
To me, at last;
The rosy nakedness of immortality,
Or something kin to that,
Has fallen over me:
I am all ecstacy,
And cannot give it words . . .

And yet they lead me off,
One upon either side,
Saying that I am mad!

RESURRECTION DAY

I hope there is a Resurrection Day
For bodies, as the greÿbeard prophets say,
When Helen's naked limbs again will gleam
Regathered from the dust of death's long dream:
When all the Olden Beauties, being fair,
Will take the watchings angels unaware,
And make God's heavenly meadows doubly sweet
With rosy vagrancy of little feet!

SHAKESPEARE

As brisk as Ariel unto Magic's Lord
Apollo and the Muses served his whim:
Her favored Singer, Nature gave to him
Seas, skies, fields, mountains for a sounding board—
His organ-stops, Man's moods of soul, mind, heart;
With apt felicities surpassing all,
Art did not tutor him but he taught Art.
The majesties of Blank Verse at his call,
Or larklike lyrics—on each instrument
He was the Master of all Song's Intent:
Night's stars are many; dawn reveals the sun
Which ushers in the glorious day alone.
Shakespeare was Shakespeare and no other one
But He could rule men from so great a throne!

THE PETTY HEART

Above your head birds use their wings
   And galleon clouds go surging by,
While you stop, fixed on petty things,
   Caught in a self-made misery.

How life affords a grand design
   The stretching constellations show
When nightfall deepens, Sign on Sign,
   And stars by many a million glow.

You think this life is all we have?—
   Then climb the heights with ardent will
Before, within a narrow grave,
   You find a pettier precinct still.

But if it is not? and you find
   A vaster realm, a larger space,
Would heaven itself suit such a mind
   Whice made God's earth a narrow place?

STRANGENESS

This living where the belted seasons flit
About the earth, upon a wandering star—
I wonder how men dare grow used to it,
Turning to custom, what is strange and far!
How can they talk, so easy, on the street
In cities and in towns, when, far and strange,
The mystery stoops down, the paraclete
Present in all that moves with time and change? . . .

Or does the strangeness stir them when they say
"Good morning" or "we might have rain today"?
Perhaps they feel the near archangels' wing
And imminence of the bright, tremendous host:
Perhaps they speak trite words to hide the thing
That walks with every heart-beat like a ghost!

BLIND

The Spring blew trumpets of Color,
   Hed Green sang in my brain:
I heard a blind man groping,
   Tap-tap, with his cane;
I pitied him his blindness,
   But can I boast I see?—
Perhaps there stands a spirit,
   Near by, who pities me;
A spirit who sees me tapping
   The five-sensed cane of mind
Amid such unguessed glory
   That I am worse than blind!

BIRD AS KING

We come by a tree
   Where one bird sings, alone,
A king of sweet power
   On melody's throne:

But, unlike a king,—
   In bright, hidden green
He sings, unattended,
   Apart, and unseen!

THE OLD FORGET

The Old forget that they were one-time young,
So ready with advice upon the tongue
To teach the Young the way they ought to go:
They should think so-and-so; do so-and-so,
And climb life like a ladder, rung by rung!

Youth's shining banner in the wind far-flung,
Youth by its instant ardors spurred and stung,
Its leaping joys so near to Age's woe,
The Old forget!

Ah, let them live before they limp, unstrung,
With weakened sinews and with half-breathed lung!—
That on the Young is morning's passing glow,
That Wonder is the way they have to go,
And that their songs must not be left unsung,
The Old forget!

THE GENTLE HERESY

You have beseiged me in the narrow street
Where I could never turn for flight,—
Caught from my warriors, little stance for feet;
All help turned into desolate faithlessness;
No bulwark left for my retreat,
No shield, for my distress!

O, Love, you terrible bowman, whose dark laugh
Sounds with your bow, and I am shot
Through; when I cry for thirst, you lift to quaff
Your bowl; but all restorative proves your wine:
No last, night-darkened epitaph,
But your new life is mine!

But since by suffering you make life for me
And never leave my heart alone,—
O, forgive, Love, the gentle heresy
Of taking oath that I will love no more,
Tasting no more your terrible mystery,—
Your rapt realms to explore!

THE DUNES

Back from the wave-carved ramparts of the beach
Skyward the gray, enormous sand-dunes reach
Stippled with far-seen trails of wandering feet
That walk up distant summits, cross, and meet
And merge into the road where lies the Town
On the small ships of which the dunes look down:
A jumble of sails and cluttered wharves and ropes
Shelved in a vista of gigantic slopes
Shining and sparkling in the burning sun . . .

The sand-fleas, helter-skelter, scurry and run
And tumble, pick-a-back; the blown grass swerves
Circling its base with graceful sweeps and curves
And arcs traced, delicate, which winds confer
Like an invisible geometer.

The ancient ocean, refluent on the shore,
Hurls, and draws back with a re-gathering roar
Its kelp and smooth-worn pebbles . . .
                              to and fro
Shuttling their legs, the little shore-birds go
Following the shining foot of every wave.
Their hunger lifts their hearts and makes them brave.

The close, warm, salty odor of the sea,
Sweet as a woman's breasts, weighs heavily
On all the air . . .
                    and now the sun goes down,
Laying its brightness on the seaward Town
A farewell space, as parting lovers meet . . .

White-purple shadows steal on crowding feet
Over the brown kelp, up the slopes that lean
Skyward . . . they touch the firs to darker green,
Into black-green: space grows to infinite height
And leads up into avenues of night
From the abrupt foot of the dunes, that seem
Causeways that climb to parapets of dream . . .

A slipping edge of disc, a tiny span,
Gleams yet, hinting the sun Leviathan;
And where the West burns like a brazier yet
Dance small, grey fisher-boats in silhouette.

The first great planet of the night hangs low,
So bright it makes our shadows as we go:
Each gulfing hollow is a haunted dell.

Now the moon, risen, casts a silver spell

In a long ocean-path . . . has a god passed
Leaving a visible way? the dunes are vast
With moonlight; every ridge, by magic, grown
A mountain under stars . . .
                                        the soul's alone,
Whipped from the body to a stellar birth
Upon another landscape (not the earth)
Banked as with solid moonlight . . .
                                        that's our moon
That was our earth . . . we walk a plenilune;
The sea is rolling silver tossed a-far . . .

We walk upon the body of a star.

I MUST CONFESS

I must confess that mine's a heart
  That ever works me wrong,
For every time I think I love,—
  A new girl comes along:

Since you have asked the very truth
  The truth must now be told—
A special gift is constancy
  For the ugly and the old!

VIGILANCE

O, you were happy, being sure
Without a thought Love would endure,
The hopes of which, so hardly wrought,
Can slide like snow, quicker than thought!
For ev'n the First Great Paradise
Was barred to Adam, in a trice . . .
It's not enough to storm a town;
  To hold it brings the great renown:
Captains who take must, after, keep
The fort, with arms which never sleep.

THE HUMAN CONUNDRUM

With the stars for his playmates, the moon, for a bride,
All the galaxies dancing at his side,
What creature lives on three breaths of air
And thrives between a curse and a prayer?

HOW FOOLISH THIS ASKING

How foolish this asking "What does life mean?"
Life's its own meaning, final and clean:
Escaping the yardstick of what's sold and bought:
Profounder than planning, deeper than thought:
Not balancing love by virtue and vice,
Nor pricing the things that lie beyond price—
Itself, without words, a sufficient reply
To the optimist's folly, the pessimist's lie!

AND SO I SMILE

I wonder if it's worth the game
To be thus affable and tame?
How often have I longed to meet
My rivals, on an empty street
Or in a meadow with a sword,
To decide who will be your lord;
Or with a pistol for a voice
To give your indecision, choice!
For I'd deal twenty deaths an hour
To rivals, if I had the power:
But poignards are no more in style,
Nor poisoned cups,—and so I smile!

THE SIMPLE TRUTH

True Love walks two by two:
    Let no vain talk deceive—
When Love has room for more,
    Then Love has room to leave!—

Though rich with all life holds
    The heart has little room
For any other flower
    But constancy's fine bloom!

STRANGE ROAD

There stood the long, white road:
    It watched him like a stranger;
Since it was new, he felt
    It must wait, thick with danger.
But night was folding in:
    With dusk's first star to mark
The Man who Feared New Roads
    Even without the Dark,
Fared forth, as fare he must!—
    He left the fading day;
The land lay, blank, about:
    He took the dim new way!
Then star on star drew forth;
    A moon brought brighter weather:
The Road reached out its hand:
    Man, Road, walked on together . . .
At last they met a lamp
    That at a window showed
To house a weary Man
    Who'd made friends with a Road!

TRIUMPH OF THE COMMONPLACE

You went where no one else dared go,
Or could, explorer,—now
The beaten path is laid
Where cowards safely tread, all unafraid,
Leading timidity like a placid cow;
The Commonplace has worked its usual wrong,
And the great song that the great poet made
Shares every idiot's tongue.

WHEN UP THE MOUNTAIN SLOPE

When up the mountain slope the shadows crawl
And the foot dares follow
Beyond each darkened hollow,
Only the topmost path is safe,
The best path for the soul—
Where there's no way down!

RONDEL OF A CHILD'S WONDER

The delight of a child in a flower
Captured me in the street;
My heart went out to its power,
As to music, soft and sweet.

It stayed my willing feet
As with a golden dower:
The delight of a child in a flower
Captured me in the street.

Let the clouds of the future lower;
I saw the paraclete
Of eternity take the hour,
Where earth and heaven meet:
The delight of a child in a flower
Captured me in the street!

EACH DAY

Each day we die a little more;
    Stale custom takes its toll:
It is the Unexpected Thing
    That brings life to the soul.

THE KING OF MEN

"The man who would be king of men,
　"We keep him in this cell:
"He says if he but held the sway,
　"With men all would be well;

"He'd abrogate all unjust laws,
　"Would banish every ill;
"But bars across his windows keep
　"Him from his 'subjects' still . . .

" 'Give me my throne that waits for me'
　"Is his continual prayer
"While he maintains his majesty
　"Upon a kitchen chair."

Then, when we halted at his door
　I heard "his Majesty" ask,
"My friend, why must you keep me here
　"From my appointed task?"

The doctor, with respectful voice
　Replied, serene and bland,—
"Because your Justice is too great,
　"As yet, you understand.

"The purest Champions of Men,
　"Have soonest gone to doom,—
"And that is why we keep you here
　"In this so little room,—

"We keep you here for all men's good:
　"Remember Athens' loss
"Through hemlock, and how Jesus Christ
　"Was murdered on His cross!

"Have patience, Sire, the day will come
　"When we can set you free:
"The fruits of Time are not yet ripe
　"For your Great Equity!—

"It will be but a while to wait;
  "Then we will let you out
"To greet the crowding multitudes
  "And hear their happy shout."

The "King" fell silent, soothed a while;
  He bowed in Monarch's pride.
The door was locked. We walked away,
  In silence, side by side.

"Perhaps? ... if you would let him out?"
  The Poet spoke in me.
The Doctor ventured a strange smile;
  Glancing aside, said he—

"In many places in the land
  "They guard such men about—
"Perhaps we'd have no worse a world
  "If they were all let out!"

YOUTH'S KINGSHIP

A weak, poor King is Youth:
  Though young days rear his throne;
Old Age, his Vizier,
  Corrupts him to the bone.

The World, his General,
  Turns on him with surprise,
And rouses up against
  His faith, a thousand lies.

He shall lie down at last
  Upon Life's harlot bed
And wake in shining day
  But to be stricken dead!

SONG'S FIRST TWO MIRACLES

In Hades Helen gave Homer Love's embrace
Because in Fame's bright Heaven he set her face,
Song's **second miracle**; Song's **first** was blind
Homer, who saw such Beauty in his mind
So that no other face has haunted men
So heavenly sweet,—nor ever shall again!

CITY OF INTOLERANCE

Let's found our City on hard intolerance,
And not on compromise that melts, half-way:
Let us dig deep, beyond the slush, sand, clay
To granite certainties where earthquakes dance
In shackles, captured in their wavering.
In the fierce sects and battles of today
It is no miserable, middling thing
That wavers, threatened! nor can music make
Firm, or some soft wish, what Today's storms shake!
And there burns but One Writing on the wall
When summits rain in fire and girders fall:
Cities that fall have been too tolerant
Of children's miseries, of grey-faced Want
Creeping in sunless tenements; civic ill
And shameless penuries that oppress men still;
The long, slow, piecemeal rot of Poverty
Where men, like sick beasts, creep to daily die:
Evils to which blind Justice grants no repeal:
These are the termites that can eat down steel
And clinch their teeth in granite, grinding to dust
The great words not made deeds in which men trust:
This is the Monstrous Writing on the Wall
That burns out, bright, before the cities fall!

TO ONE WHO SAID HE WAS BORED WITH LIFE

It bores you, then, to live and die
　　Upon this cloud-scarfed ball
That drops from space to space of sky
　　In an eternal fall?

With the great heavens drawn above,
　　Beneath, the wondrous earth,
How strange is life, how strange is love,
　　And death, that walks with birth . . .

O, when I die, say I lived ill,
　　Say that my days were poured
Like wasted wine, say all you will,
　　But never, "Kemp was bored!"

DUNE-REVENANT

I said "when I'm alive no more
　　"And my soul at last goes free,
"You'll find me walking on the dunes
　　"And down beside the sea.
"So, if you glimpse a wavering form,
　　"Or front a vanishing face,
"You'll know that I've come back once more
　　"To my accustomed place!"

The City Summer keeps me here,
　　But, a wonder to relate,
Last night I more than dreamed I stood
　　In front of a great wave's spate;
My longing was so strong I found
　　Myself by sand and tide:
I'm sure a coastguard met me there—
　　And spread the news I'd died!

BRIGHT DAY'S QUERY

On days like this none asks what life is for,
But is content to be; the sailboat's wake,
The splashes that the dipping seabirds make,
Speak life rich with contentment to the core;
The long, soft seas that roll and plunge and break
Fill the bright day with sound; lapsed leagues of shore
Glimmer till sight grows dim where the waves shake
High plumes of brightness. Why can't all men have
A place like this to make their lives more brave
Here where each clean wave on the other rolls?—
Why must the crowded city crush their souls?—

LORDS OF DREAM

He who is Lord of a Dream
Can move both time and tide—
He who is Lord of a Dream
Is Lord of all else beside:
The Opener of the Gate,
On him the people wait.
He who is Lord of a Dream
Can take up in his hand
What at first is a little sand:—
Cast into the day-beam,
It will grow a mighty land . . .
But if he leave his faith
Nothing will he obtain
But a broken stalk
Rotten in the rain.
Though kind to earth the shower
Rain rots the rootless flower,
And all the bright leaves blanch
Upon the rent-off branch!

APOLOGY TO ST. FRANCIS

Saint Francis, I am sorry
  That I have gone apart
From that deep lore you fathomed
  With plummet-line of heart.

Once, through three leaks, now covered,
  Sweet rain spun, silver-thin;
Once, through a broken window,
  A surprised bird flew in;

The sun, a brother to me,
  Stood close, there being no pane,—
The breaks re-placed, both sun and moon
  Shine, orbs aloof, again . . .

O, give me once more your hillside
  With grass to lean upon,
The moon, once more my sister,
  And my bride, the Naked Dawn!

The sunset is my window
  That looks on God's domain;
My Mother of God, she is the Moon;
  My Magdalen is Rain!

SALVAGE

I cannot answer why I came to be bereft
Of Hands. There dropped a gale. The waters burst like smoke.
And then I found myself abandoned to the seas.
My sails flapped rent to rags where adverse thunders broke.
But good ships have a heart as strong as their own oak.

I had no one to steer: and yet I put about.
I stood up to the wind. I found the sea more kind
Than those so small of soul they left me for the boats;
So good a ship as I, with such sure skill designed.
With horror I beheld the Captain drop behind.

Then resolution gripped my beams from stem to stern.
My figurehead resolved that it would lend me sight.
Ten storms worse than that first, they raked me fore and aft.
I trod on through the day, I drove on through the night:
I held an even keel in every gale's despite.

My cargo, too, was good; for half around the world
Another continent was crying for its need.
Some instinct given to ships woke lively through my boards,
That without mate or crew vouchsafed me to proceed . . .
My courage cries for help. All full-manned ships, give heed!

If you can spare some men to rig a jury-mast
And dare for a reward, greater than gold will be
(Though there'll be bags of that!) your uncoined recompense:
A conscience sound as oak, commending bravery
That saved a sturdy ship abandoned, thus, at sea!

THE TIDE

Goes in and out with its gigantic tread
The tide, a beast fastidious of its bed.
It waddles up like Behemoth from the Deep,
To search the shelving shallows for its sleep,
Then, with far trampling, it draws back again . . .

It teems with hordes for watching fishermen
That wait about the cluttered wharves of the Town,
Or push out where the nets are studded down . . .

The pitchforked fish, obscene white bellies up,
Hurled out as worthless (that the gulls may sup,
Screaming and wheeling in coveys), lard the drift.
The anchored boats against the current lift,
Or lie, sidecast, on endless levels of sand;
The bay seems here begotten of the land,
The land—of sea and sky!   Chaos spawns all!

Along the ooze primordial creatures sprawl:
Things carrying shells for house; blind lives that put
The body forth, transmuted to a foot;
Flanged, steel-blue sea-worms, ribbons that reach and draw;
Small monsters born of life's first groping law,
Embryons all eye set drifting; creatures rare
That run like clocks in crystal; some as fair
As naked beauty's self, whose forms transgress
The general norm of primal ugliness,
Wave sapphire fringes, sail with shining sails,
Sconce gleaming bodies in laced and exquisite grails . . .

For the old blind slime again gets motion here
Where life's first efforts into being peer
Still; and where, blank and raw to wind and sun,
The ravels of the First Creation run!

SEA-APPROACH

As cities where we are not seem
Thronged with the people of a dream—
Like a deep voice far underground,
Remote and dreamlike yet profound,
Thus, long before we reach the shore
We catch the ocean's unseen roar
Before it bursts upon the eye
Incredibly brimming all the sky,
Half-beggaring infinity!—
Where we perceive the spouting whale,
The steamer's smoke, the leaning sail,—
And tiny shells of delicate grail—

So, wondrous and afar, we sense
The enigmas of omnipotence,
The Power that thinks by worlds, yet still
Accepts the smallest atom's thrill,
Which fearful residence doth maintain
In Shakespeare's or an idiot's brain!

PARTITIONS

It is the sceptic's glory to deny,
    The heart's crown to accept and to believe
Until the inner sight's reality
    Sees what no reason-clouded eyes perceive:
The wonder of strict limits seeming frail
    Dividing into parts created space
Down to the distinctness of the tiniest grail
    That rounds the smallest insect's golden grace.
When with His compass God creation spanned
    His Order circumscribed Enormity:
Who is not glad the pale, small intimate sand
    Keeps back the vast disaster of the sea?

EARTH HAS FAITH

There comes upon my roof rain sweet with heaven,
Rain washing clean the world in Spring's baptism;
Endowing once again with magic chrism
The hidden, ardent growth; this is the leaven
Leavening all: earth's dreariness has faith,
Still, in the face of what seems imminent death
Looking up gladly at the dangerous sky,—
Yes, earth has faith that good days justify:
Yes, earth has faith each Spring then why not I?

UPON THE SAND

Upon the sand the slant rain falls in vain,
The multitudes of the arrows of the rain;
The long, grey shores sprout cruelty, and the sand
Creeps on, forever marching against the land
That would be fertile and fat with ordered peace
If these invasions from the sea would cease . . .
Upon the sand the slant rain falls in vain,
Futile are the invasions of the rain.
There lies no end nor terminus to the sand
Sloping its million spears against the land
Or innumerably streaming in charges blind
And terrible, on the little horses of the wind.
And though each bent blade seems to thwart their course,
It only shifts the pattern of their force—
Innumerably they begin again,
Grain on enlisted, diamond-helmeted grain,
Overwhelming the armies of the rain . . .
Only a bitter black marsh here and there
With a snake-mottled flower savage-fair,
Or speargrass naked in the wind's caress
Pricks space in universal barrenness.

SONG OF LIGHT

I heard the lingering morning star
Playing with sweet and silver power;
Then Dawn caught on its golden lyre
The song lost by the morning star.
All day I heard the golden song
Of light and splendor. All day long
The sun gave music to my heart
In which the dancing waves took part.
The orchestral sunset's harmony
Poured music on the West for me.
The moon took up her song of light
Giving her music to the night
Where not a single discord mars
The diapasons of the stars.

THE GODDESS CLOACINA

They worshipped the goddess Cloacina, through
An outdoor toilet as her altar, going
To it, often, through rain; with rain on their heads
Tending to Nature's offices. Their jakes
Was an affair open to naked air
An hupaithraic temple made of boards
With an old blanket nailed across
The entrance, for a door—
They could look out on sea and sky
And observe the seagulls gliding by!

REVEILLE

So easy to make glorious or betray,
Bright day unmarred, what shall be done with you?—
Day before Dark a great or doleful day:
To be remembered as a shining view
Of Heaven's steadfast zenith breaking through,
Or as thick darkness gathered to betray
Credulity of fools that lose their way,
Led sheeplike off some false, precipitous view.

But let this flattery to the thought be laid:
Stumbling or riding straight to gain the goal,
It bides a certain comfort to the soul
To know that Justice like a peak shall stand,
God's sun upon her, at the Truth's right hand,
And that Man's life is finally not betrayed!

TO A SHIP'S FIGUREHEAD

They've set you, with your cracked and wooden stare,
Above a doorway; you who used to fare
Walking across the seas before they drove
Asunder, where your vessel's body clove.
Now yours is green-sloped lawn and careful tree,
And hedge the gardener's shears clip formally;
While bachelor buttons, pansies in a row,
Make prim with bloom the ordered plots below
I wonder how men dared to set you here?—
Yet could it be I read a sturdy cheer
Where your each seam lets sun and shadow in
From battered forehead to grim, broken chin?
And could it be your blank eyes gladly find
Some naked wonder to which ours are blind?—
I read in you a passion to approve
That discipline that drives the ordered groove:
For when you sought the stars you also led
A Captain's will that sent your course ahead,
And a resolve that bore you through the storm
Where peril clung by each sky-climbing form.

It seems that you have made that house your ship
To voyage on where winds of spirit whip:
So such as dwell beneath you must conceive
Anchors for doubt beyond all flaws that grieve,
Shipshape behaviours, hands which, mutual, lend
Help where enduring courage proves staunch friend
Of enterprise, despite the gales that break
Where the ship drives her white, enormous wake.
While Life still goes about her Great Affair
Despite the cynic's bite, the sceptic's flair,
It seems you're no unuseful ornament
But fill, somehow, your Maker's first intent!

WHEN I THINK OF ALL THE SHIPS

When I think of all the great ships
   That have gone down at sea
To lie along the bottom sands
   Till time shall cease to be,
With captains in the cabins
   And slaves that sleep in rows,
And dainty skeleton ladies
   In ruffs and furbelows—
O, then I wish the ocean
   Was a thing that had not been
Because of all the lives and ships
   That have been lost therein . . .

When I think of all the glorious lads
   That have been drowned at sea
Or have perished cluttered on a raft
   In its immensity,
Or, cast up on a wave-washed rock,
   Ringed 'round with creeping foam,
Have crouched in clouds of crying gulls
   Until their souls went home—
O, then I wish the ocean
   Was a thing God had not made
To set about ten thousand shores
   Its infinite ambuscade.

Yet every time I see a ship
   Go dwindling far to sea,
In spite of all its deaths, I'm glad
   For its waters rolling free
Where men may learn that courage
   Is more than precious stones,
That the soul is more forever
   Than its house of flesh and bones:
For the glory of the greatened man
   That its wars and waves have built
I am glad God poured the ocean
   Like a thing the sky has spilt!

SONG FOR SHIP-BUILDERS

I celebrate the Building of The Ship
More than her crowded launching, flags a-whip;
Though certainly there is no other thing
Quite like this, but the roar 'round a new king—
Where waves walk foaming up and rush back streaming
Along a sentient thing of noblest fettle,
With far, reverberant echoes, whistles screaming,
And cheering folk to watch her ride and settle.

I sing the slow achievement of the ship,
And not the shouting and the celebration
Poets have rhymed, of every time and nation.
I sing the delicate plumb-line dropping sheer,
The bolts that take their firm, allotted grip,
The bent, leviathan ribs, the fashioned gear
That wed, close-woven, till she's full-created . . .
Before her launching comes, by multitudes feted,
And she is sent down foaming ways, to be
The mistress of the cloud and wind and sea—
Before she knows the launched, increasing motion
That gives her to the unceasing, vast, green ocean;
Before she's ready for the Five Seas' going
Wherever the nervous compass guides her way,
Where, lightning-edged, the bent, black palm leans, blowing,
Or where white icebergs daunt the North's dark day,—
Long back of her must live the imagination,
The blueprint's capture of the dream's creation;
And after that must thrive the hard, skilled trouble,
The annealing fires, the cauldroned pitch a-bubble;
Years back of these, the patience of invention,
The balanced figures' finest calculation,
And all the heart-breaks that forecast Prevailing,
(Aye, and all crafts that ever have gone sailing)
Before the Ship looms fit for Life's intention!

KEEPING UP PRICES

The sparkling waves were swept as if a wind
Walked suddenly: the sea was thousand-finned
Where, up the swell, unnumbered backs were creeping
In drifting stars; but fishermen stood about
The docks and decks as if their eyes were sleeping,
As slack of soul as any corner lout,
As idle as a sail upon a spar
Of some lost ship whose last watch none is keeping,—
With aimless drifting for a guiding star!—
Victims as of intangible defeat,
Inaction gripped the restless souls of men.
Now, moved by hopeless instinct for their work
And half-ashamed conditions made them shirk
The fishermen acted guilty, shifting feet:
But they remembered prices were too low
So they must let the schools of mackerel go:
Who only yesterday could not afford
To bring in fish that they dumped overboard!

BASIC NECESSITIES

I'll crave a board or two to turn the wind
Where the brown, barren sand finds the grass thinned;
A roof above that leaks a little rain;
And shy dawn at a broken window pane.
I'll choose a book or so before I go,
Food for a poet's heart and active brain,
Of gracile Greek and Latin grave and slow,
To grace the shelves I've built against the wall.
There I can face whatever may befall:

Frigid decorum will not pursue me there,
The worldling's strut, nor the proud Pharisee's air;
The goose-brained critic's gibe I'll never miss . . .
Perhaps I'll find a girl or two to kiss—

For I'm your graceless rascal gracefully
Weaving some sundry lines to get renown,
While putting all my fame to jeopardy
As amorous persuasion's easiest clown.

OLD FOOLS' HOLIDAY

Cackling, they crept beneath the moon,
    A ribald song was sung:
Each old man looked, in the slanting light,
    Like a black dot on a prong.
It should have scared their souls to thought;
    Instead, they hopped away
Along the haunted, moonwhite road
    On an old fools' holiday.
A door that seethed with open light
    Waked, in the night, alone;
The droning drums and flutes began
    And moaning saxophone.
They entered in; a wreath was thrust
    Upon each gangling head—
Three lurching shadows on the wall
    Three words for shadows said . . .
They pounded on the board for drinks
    And greedy drinks were brought
That sparkled with the gift that each
    Was quite the man he thought . . .
It is a tawdry tale to tell
    That's cleaner hastened by,
Of limping shank and shrunken haunch
    That paired a young girl's thigh,
While gyrant age remembered wives
    That soon would wield a tongue
To dart, "that's what an old fool gets
    "For thinking to play young!" . . .
It is a ghastly rhyme to spin.
    How, falling now and then,
Along the sick, forewarning moon
    Those grey lads homed again:
Each knew a rusty joint a-creak
    Like an old gate on a hinge—
Each felt already, in his thought,
    That fresh rheumatic twinge! . . .

Was that a trumpet that they heard?
  What was that thickening glare
That walked against the eastern sky
  Like a red ghost up a stair?—
For it seemed to them the Judgement Day
  Broke, on the palsied night
As soaring, clotted flakes from hell
  Fumed slowly up to sight:—
Though to all else the rose-kissed clouds
  Of morning had begun;
While Youth, the jubilant, golden Cock,
  Crowed, loud, against the sun!

LI PO FULFILLS HIS HOROSCOPE

For old Li Po, the Chinese bard,
Song without wine came rather hard;
And if there was a girl or two
Completer still the music grew . . .
Because the stars said in the sky
Of drinking water he would die
Unto a circling, gurgling sound
Without a single girl around,—
To thwart the foreordained design
Li's only drink was cups of wine:
In girls and wine he did abound;
In wine, love, and the lute's sweet sound:
While skillful brush and burning mind
Put all the younger bards behind;
And when the last word stood in view,
The poem was a painting too,
With lovely curve and sweeping stress
For which kings made their treasures less,
And lords gave jewels to possess.
Secure in fame and great in pride
And sure at last of stars belied
When old, still drinking late and soon,
Li fell in love with the young moon!
Wooing her one night from a boat
He leaped to kiss her bared, white throat:
And, finding water all around,
And no girl with her zone unbound,
He sank, dismayed, without a sound
Except that made by waters, sped
In soft relapse above his head!

FISHERMEN

When stars still gather, height on height,
    Beneath the mighty Milky Way—
They put forth in the utter night
    Before the first, faint flush of day,

To gather in the quiet nets
    That wait, black-laced, against the sky—
Which the first touch in tumult sets
    With surging life that would not die!

They are the huntsmen of the sea:
    They chase the bright and rippling herds
That roam its dark immensity
    Watched over by the ocean's birds.
Far off, as if it were the wind,
    Brightening the surface, they behold
Ten thousand mackerel, silver-finned,
    That run in wavering banks of gold!

DAWN—CAPE COD

Before the day's creation is begun
I must go forth to meet the unseen sun—
Out on the hushed, expectant flats I love,
More lone because of the still sky above.
The village houses lie like herds asleep.
The tide, black-burnished, spreads out, flat and deep.
There walks a wind of coming change abroad . . .
The sun shows like a traveller down a road.

Then—what the dark reserved unseen before—
I see long, dancing golden slopes of shore . . .
Then, as I walk back, close, to left and right,
I find young summer in full tides of green;
Where flickering branches thwart the morning lean:
Leaves touch my face, leaves brush against my hand,
And beach plums bloom in little banks of white
Up slopes of infinite, immaculate sand.

TERRIBLE ARE DELICATE THINGS

For terrible are delicate things.
Tell me not of the crash of war:
The glimpse of the soft evening star,
The little airs that morning brings
Shake the soul where earthquakes fail.
The young moon clad in silver mail,
The sigh of love upon the breast,—
These more the hearts of men molest!

TRIBUTE TO YOUTH

This only have I learned by growing old:
That Youth was right, as it will always be:
Each year increases this one faith in me,
Driving with power that may not be controlled.
I give its full sail to the wind unrolled,
And join the onward motion of its sea.
Continuing in supreme felicity
Its banners lead me on, with victory scrolled.

Dull would I be and old in heart and thought
(I cannot help the years) if once I failed
To hail this wisdom that long life has brought.
Still Young Occasion, instant in command,
Takes Dauntless Resolution by the hand:
Youth, thank the gods, Youth always has prevailed!

LATE FLOWERING

A gnarled and knobbed encumbrance on the land
Was that old apple tree whose time seemed done.
Young branches lifted strong on every hand
Where husbandry strove hard for profits won
And every stony rood for gain seemed planned.
When lustier growths might freshen in the sun
I wondered why the owner let it stand:
The old tree yielded scanty fruit or none!

Then Spring, miraculous with red and green
And shining gold, revealed the reason why:
Blossoms so thick they gave no space between
White as belief in immortality
Transformed that tree: may life to me allow
As I grow old, such brightness on the bough!

POET'S CONFESSION

I married Song full early: I have gone
Down Song's ways all my days; Song is to me
Forever a supreme felicity
Like a continuance of undying dawn.
The world regards me as a life undone
Because I've left men's staid economy
To keep the morning stars' first ecstacy—
Yes, for my ways of life much blame I've won.

Yet I stood firm though I felt untold weight
Upon me: for the music of the spheres
Lifted me to the stars with sure control:
For still, midmost the discords of Man's years,
Music's immortal heartbreak takes my soul.

NATURAL DIRT

O, felicitous, natural dirt.
O, the healthy feet of children pushing through the dust,
Wading through puddles.

TINY MISSIONS

The tiny, multitudinous missions of the ants
On dusty safaris;
The little scouts ascending grassblades
For further path-finding.

GOSSAMER

Riding with the ever-restless, never-resting wind
That, in its gentler moods,
Is carrying little spiders through the air
Buoyed on their gossamers.

OCEAN SUNSET

I'm amazed at the impudence
Of these insignificant clouds
Which, before the night begins,
Gather, and grow intense
Above the departing sun
Just as the day is done.
One cloud reels drunk on gold,
One gets all drenched in a hue
That is half a diamond and half
The evening's enormous blue . . .
Three cachinnant seagulls laugh
At what I'm laughing at, too!
For they're boasting, those poor little clouds,
That those ships of color are theirs,—
Though, until they are full of some star
Like the sun, they're but drab affairs:
While the sun departs, they prevail,
Each a god in golden mail;
Couched in the sun's last smile,
A divine effulgence a while;
Then their borrowed wonder thins
As day's last glory is furled
And the smoke of the night begins
Pouring up and over the world!

A WOMAN'S LIPS AND LOVE

Better than gold by far,
  Glory, and crowded ships,
Or victory after war—
  The kiss of a woman's lips!

Let sunsets darken and fold,
  Let glory and gold depart:
Better than glory or gold
  The love in a woman's heart!

FOREVER THE HINTS

The dawn-star treads the Dark!
It dimly silvers the tide.
Three surprised clouds stand by;
Four startled gulls take the sky.

From a far-edged, rosy mark
The fire-flaked dawn wakes wide
Or ever there is a sun
Or day itself is begun
And plenitudes of light
Embosom accustomed sight!

Its canvas and masts distinct,
Its cordage golden-linked,
One fisher-boat stands across
The lambent disc of the day . . .

The heart of unbelief
Cannot forego its brief
Instinct to bow and pray—
While the sun climbs, small to discern
With its edge just seen on the sky
Before it stands widened and high—
And the little boat trudges on;
Forever the hints return
Of The Light Of A Greater Dawn!

LITTLE TALK

He left his small town that he might escape
The wry-mouthed gossip and the little talk—
With Great Minds and Great Souls to think and walk
Where human destiny takes a vaster shape.
Dismayed, he found the giants cast a shade
With the same lack of sun the pigmies made.
Cynic of cynics, then, his teeth on edge,
He shunned ancestral wine without the pledge:
From men of name and fame he walked apart,—
And none dared ask what sickness ate his heart! . . .
And when he came to die, like a sick child
He turned his face against the silent wall—
His soul was tired of every bugle-call;
The last illusion left him unbeguiled.
He scorned the priests, refusing heaven's joy:
Would not God boast of Christ, His sturdy Boy?
And seraphim, still feeling Satan's scars,
Be rife with little talk about Old Wars?

'WARE DERELICT

I am drifting, I am lifting with the tide,
I have no will nor object of my own.
With barnacles and weeds I'm over-grown,
And in the burning day my seams gape wide.
The waters can no more come in upon me,
For washing level with the waves I ride!
My ensign, whipped to rags, has long foregone me,—
I have forgotten that I once had pride!
With bergs and barren drifts I keep my dance;
The blood-red sun sets, weary; it shines, old;
Upon me lapses morning's faded gold;
The dreadful light of stars sheds no romance
Upon my aimless, long, ignoble going—
For my last dream has left with my last chance:
What do I care what wind is slack or blowing,
Or how the storms retreat or tides advance?
And glad I am I have no pity more
For gallant craft that run on me, unseen;—
No longer caring for what things have been,
I take them in the dark; and, to the core
Thrust my black bulk and dreadful brokenness,
Surprising with rich ruin some bare shore,
Till the sea's going boasts one token less
Of what the hopes of men are striving for!

SELF-PITY

Where Hell on Purgatory opens out
There lies a region Dante did not see,
Or if he did, he did not tell about,—
Perhaps because of its dubiety.
Damned by themselves the feeble wretches spin;
There vague self-pitiers hug their misery;
All they can see, with blear eyes turned within,
Are their small hearts shrivelled like winter gourds;
All they can hear—their own weak, whining words!
And all they say (their tongues are never still)
Is how unfairly they have suffered ill!
Each of them walks as on a reeling ball
That whirls upon one spot nor moves along—
They move indeed but go nowhere at all!
Life's strength they spend in being weak, not strong;
Back they must mount and spin, each time they fall!—
And this with sad perversity they do
In pertinacious punishment self-sought
Beyond all hope of help, all strength of thought,
Past self-reliance and its bugle-call!—
By which the honest lesson must be taught
Self-pity is the meanest vice of all!

THE JUDGEMENT OVER-PASSED

The nations feared that morning when it came
And the sky's tenuous shell was rimmed with fire;
From North to South, from East to smoky West
A ring of fate upon men's spirits pressed;
Like the air crowding space which still leaves room,
The emptiness of day grew full of doom;
And something like a constant-twanging wire
Brought rising discord with a hint of flame
Mid-day stood scarlet like a cheek of shame;
Then chasmed West was lurid-gashed with red
Like sunset on Mount Sinai when the Lord
Threatened the People of His Choice with dread:
The granaries of His Wrath to bursting stored!
The zig-zag lightnings, ragged overhead,
Flashed golden wings, while lagging thunders roared.
So, when the day they feared would be their last
Into the limbo of survived things passed
Like empty, bitter cups put by, once quaffed,—
Men clapped each other on the back, and laughed:
"God!—what a day!" they said,
Not knowing they were dead!—
Because on shore the ocean did not run,
Because they saw no angel in the sun,—
Like ghouls that cannot smell their own decay,
Men did not know **they'd passed the Judgement Day!**

INSTINCT OF THE PATH

Long after the forgotten feet have passed
The instinct of the trodden path remains
Where nothing but direction seems to last.
Weeds cannot stay there; it's not washed by rains
Back to oblivion; through the boles, thick-massed
It looks for open space where heart's faith gains
Deliverance breaking forth from briars and weeds
To where again the road of life proceeds!

The heart's path leads men, if they'll only go
In faith along it, though it seems but slow:
Those that see little think the heart is blind;
Yet through the twilight of the boughs above
From their lost wildernesses of the mind,
The heart's path leads men back to trust and love!

I OFTEN THINK

I often think
That, one of these days,
One of these trails
Will break out, and open, flush,
On the Old Garden of Eden,
And we'll find
God, Adam and Eve
All out walking there,
Taking the morning air!

POETS AS MAP-MAKERS

Despite cartography their passion is
To find in barest maps a richer bliss
Than sober boundaries, proper sites to draw:
Their maps show emerald cities without flaw;
Where Troy burns, vanquished by a woman's kiss;
Here fabled lands which seldom travellers saw
Keep no frontiers to poets' ecstacies;
Here wait the Seven Cities of Cibola;
Here golden India stands against the sun
Next naked isles of spice and cinnamon:
Hence generations of successive youth,
Made glorious with the passion and the pain
Where still the Phoenix shines, the Greater Truth,
Resume Arabia and her fires' disdain!

REAL ESTATE

To vend and barter
The world of God!—
We, God's squatters,
To put up for a price
Grass-rippling meadows,
And the lissome, sweet bodies
Of leaf-blown trees
So full of gracefulness
And lusty with green . . .
O, you piddling fools,
Go down to your graves
And let your bones
Be sold with your land!

A POET HAUNTED

A poet, haunted with all delicate things,
Would weave some music of them: he is fain
Of the fine, luminous air that speeds far wings;
Of exquisite lines of light that daunt the rain;
Of frost's bright labyrinths on the morning pane;
Of leaves' unfoldings with such tints embossed
As Masters tremble on, but seldom gain—
Without these all this busy world were lost!—

Of Youth's dared days like new crowns on young kings;
Whom rightly no persuasions can contain;
Of music murmuring from lapsing strings;
Of clouds' last glories in the hushed inane—
Hoarders which spend, where nothing must remain,—
To fill starved usury at one frenzied cost;
Of twilights where the little winds complain,—
Without these all this busy world were lost!

The morning star its wavering lucence flings,
Surprising with the rose's ghost, the Main;
Ah, one small bird, like Melancholy, sings
Of how Love, with a trident and a seine,
All naked else, in bright, immortal pain,
Snares Romeo's, Juliet's brief, wild passion crossed
For glorious shame to Age's cold disdain:
Without these, all this busy world were lost!

Beyond such insubstantial things, what gain?
O, hearts of men on life's dark tumults tossed—
O, honey that is fed on crumbs of bane,—
Without these, all our busy world were lost!

WORLD OF BIRDS

Above our world there stands a world of trees
    Where leaf-embowered songsters build their nests,
Birds that wear crimson scarves about their throats
    And colors from the sunrise on their breasts.

They move and dip among their kinsmen leaves;
    As bright and buoyant as the leaves are they,
Waiting, half-hid, for Light's first baton-stroke
    To bid them hail with song the break of day!

MY BOOKS

My books are ragged veterans
    Much leaked on, in my shack:
But each of them's bound with a rainbow
    And wears glory on its back.

THE REAL WORLD

(Centuries of Bards and Heroes)
Crowds and motions are around me
　　When I seem the most alone;
Chains of time are loosed that bound me
　　And I come into my own.
Centuries of bards and heroes
　　Throng the palace of my dreams;
Sometimes I suspect the Real
　　Is like this: all else but seems.
All the little, silly troubles
　　Like a mist-wraith fade away
While the Laurelled and Heroic
　　Touch me with eternal day!

LOVE'S VIGILANCE

O, you were happy, being sure
Without a thought Love would endure,
The hopes of which, so hardly wrought,
Can slide like snow, quicker than thought!
For ev'n the First Great Paradise
Was barred to Adam, in a trice . . .

It's not enough to storm a town:
To hold it brings the great renown:
Captains who take must, after, keep
The fort with arms which never sleep!

WINE-DRINKERS' SONG
(For Bob Hanley, at Tony's on Mcdougal Street)

We are drinking wine tonight;
   But a little while ago
We were all tied up in knots,—
   Now we feel a genial glow;
Tolerant of each man's truth
We regain life's first gift, Youth!

All our hates dissolve to love,
   All our enemies turn friends,—
And for every ill deed done
   We resolve to make amends:
Every wrong must bend to right:
We are drinking wine tonight.

But not deeply in our cups
   Must we let ourselves depart:
Just enough to light the mind,
   And to lend warmth to the heart
Will we drink, so an ill end
May not intervene, my friend!

We'll allow no small dispute
   To obtrude upon the scene,
No poor, trivial thing, grown great,
   'Midst our joy to intervene;
Not a minute will we let
Words to pass we might regret . . .

When we wend our homeward way
   We'll be glad no silly wrath
Waking sick, forgotten things,
   Casts a shadow on our path,—
We'll remember with delight,
That we drank good wine, this night!

I HAVE FOUND OUT

I have found out in love a little flattery
Turns out much better than assault and battery.

THE ABSURD, GLORIOUS FABLES

The absurd, glorious fables of the gods
Truer than truths set down in periods
Of barren words: rather Jove's monstrous scrapes
And Mercury's devious shifts and deft escapes,
The allegories sitting in the stars;
The beasts of heaven, from the war-god Mars
And rosy, liquid Venus, to the Bull,
And Bears, both Great and Little, standing full
Across the zenith—Orion with the Sword,
And all of Paganism's lusty horde!

THE INNER SATISFACTION

The Inner Satisfaction is the goal;
There is no other profit for the soul:
In palace or in hut if you abide,
It does not matter—**with that gift inside!**

STEPS TO APPOLO

The Poet is no child of easy chance,—
He only wins whose ecstacy endures
Beyond a thousand traps, a thousand lures;
Past luring moments of soft-eyed romance
Of neither courage nor continuance.
From stress and trial the power you seek grows yours,
From star-touched falls that flight itself assures.
With thunder and with fire the planets dance!

For if you battle with all lacks and wants,
The singing heart that nothing ever daunts,
The ever and increasing great delight
Will find you, as a star glides down the night.

Reach upward, hard!—a Strong Immortal Hand
Will reach down, taking yours: and you will stand!

TO THE WINGED MUSES

You girls who've got wings on your back,
Delighting daughters of song,—
As the winds beat a shining track
Along the dancing grass
Or brighten over the sea—
So you come, so you pass,
Giving this song to me
Just before you are gone!

So all things good come to men:
The sail takes a flash from the sun,
The sail shifts, blank again.
Spending's the worth of gold
That misers in vain do hold!
O, the singer that seeks to prolong
A song, a drink, or a kiss
Loses what worth there is
In kissing, wine, or a song!

FAITH IN IMMORTALITY

Against what makes a billion ghosts
　　And leaves no man alive
Unaided by angelic hosts
　　How can one think to strive?

Let time be little, then, to me
　　But what my hopes conceive
Beyond the wakening flower and tree
　　And summer's brief reprieve:

Haunted by things I barely guess,
　　I try to shape in rhyme
A hint of Everlastingness
　　That is not slain by Time!

THE GREY DAY

I quite agree not even the elect
Could of their favoring deity expect
　　Each day to be a fair day;
And I was yet a boy when I discerned
The thing that rapturously the poet learned
　　About June and its rare day.
I know it would be very rash of me,
Or anyone, to ask each day to be
　　A heyday, May-day, play-day;
I grant behind the clouds the sun shines still—
But, use whatever dulcet phrase you will—
　　A grey day's still a grey day!

SHELLEY'S IS HAMLET'S CLOUD

What is a cloud?—I do not know
   Any more than Shelley did,
Except it makes no constant show,
   Being the eyes' ephemerid
Where imagination's bliss
Lies in metamorphosis.

Hamlet jibed Polonius
   With this query of a cloud
Whose jocoseness must discuss
   All that fantasy allowed—
Hamlet and Shelley intertwined
Weave the Poet's rainbowed mind!—

MY MIND'S A TRAMP

My Mind, you are such a tramp,
   Always gadding about,
And often bringing me thoughts
   I might do better without.

And yet perhaps I am wrong,
   For it's often fun, I agree,
To find all the world's out of step
   Excepting you and me!

HUMAN TRUST

Here's to Hope, and then, to Love,—
   Two prime passions of the soul,
May you their fulfillment prove
   As from a replenished bowl:

Hope can widen any street,
   Love can clear the darkest blame,
And where honest spirits meet
   Flowers spring that need no name.

Summer's blossoms spring and fade,
   But the flowers of human trust
Are from such a substance made
   That they never fall to dust!

MACHIAVELLI

To honest folk of headlong thought
Urgent for good though gained through ill
When History's First Sophist taught
That the end justifies the means,
The Devil laughed behind the scenes
And the heart of God stood still.

The tree of knowledge once so very sweet
Is now a common weed on every street.

THE GREATEST ENEMY

He drew too close for any blow to reach,
  Like a skilled boxer—yet he was as far
As where like giant flowers the systems pleach,
  Bewildered blossoming of star on star.

I could not reason with him, for my ear
  Was his. He stole the honey from my tongue,
My foeman, near as my own heart was near
  Whose strength against me never lay unstrung.

And God could not deliver me from him,
  Nor could I buy him off: he scorned all pelf—
He takes my last blood as my eyes grow dim,
  That greatest enemy of myself—**myself!**

MINOR PROPHET

**For if one serve a dream, he must be true
Unto that dream, or be to life untrue!**
So I must tell them how I saw them go
Shackled with everything that was not so:
Surely amid full day how groped mankind
With fierce, false lies that darkened heart and mind.
"Speak to them not: for they will give small heed;
"Show them your heart, and they will make it bleed!
"Greater than you have tried the task before
"And have accepted a reward full sore!"
"If greater ones than I have seen and told
"In vain: I'll not be silent, but more bold!
"The prophet's voice naught but himself restrains:
"When I see people wearing needless chains!—"
Then my voice fell: I gave an inward groan;
For, looking down, I saw I bore my own!

REVENGE

He sought revenge for a remembered slight,
He was led on by hatred for a light.
He should have feared his goal, and turned aside;
But now he must keep on, from bitter pride;
His whole aim lengthened forward to that hour
When brooded blows would fatten his despite
Upon his enemy. Opportunity came:
When, what was this that burst in dreaded flower?—
Hate's sure destruction, cherished by his flame,
Clove him, instead: a doom divinely meet!
His long revenge brought down his own defeat,
Revenge, the slave's misguided dream of power:
The lightning fell, invoked by his dark trust.
The Man himself lay darkened in the dust!

DEATH OF THE GENTLE HORSE-THIEF

While with a storm of light the dawn broke wide
He rode a stolen horse that grew his pride;
The horse he rode with his mind grew so like,
The gentlest rein he used, no spur need strike.
Why, in a world where most is sold and bought,
Must this man lack this horse and turn its thief?
They rode as if God made them with one thought;
While grim relays of speed down nights and days,
And broken trails referred to feathered chief
And tracking scout, still led pursuit its maze . . .
The man could feel fresh dangers gaining on
His fears, a little more with each slow dawn.
Since Order with Disorder still must cope,—
Like all whose desperation is their hope,
The thief wore muffled haste about his neck
Until his haste became a waiting rope:
But, sharing feeling with the horse beneath,
He hadn't heart to ride his friend to death!—
And then, through his kind comradeship, the wreck
Of substance fell from under; and his feet
Found dreadful void to step on; and his plight
Brought him, a climbing antic, bolt-upright:
Then made his agile body no more fleet.
Men left it for the carrion birds' delight
Rhythmically winding in the midmost air,
While all the West breathed sunset like a prayer!

THE MACHINES

Can any soft, smooth, lapidarian rhyme
With these gigantic dynamoes keep time?
Can any rhymer's mastery assume
The surge and thunder of the engine room?
Here are machines with strange, small, metal faces
That lift up shouldering thunder with sure traces,
And pull our townships, cities, states along!—
As strong as rivers and as tides are strong;
Whose backs are sloped in steel; whose bulbs are eyes;
Athletic oil shines on whose pliant thighs;
Who bit the lightning in their adamant lips,
And come with all Niagara to grips;
Whose whistle unto sterterous whistle calls:
A few men move about in overalls,
Testing, adjusting, watching to and fro:
Listening to their future as they go!

HELEN IN HADES

All that I sought was peace and happiness,
But there was something fatal in my eyes
And maddening in my mouth; men grew unwise
And crazed, beholding me, and Law was less
Than their desire; one vagrant, windy tress,
Or my unguarded bosom's rich surprise
Filled each man's heart with visions and vain cries
And his arms rose in dreams for my caress.

Yea, I saw neither happiness nor peace
But hungry faces bright as swords and spears;
I was the White, Unwilling Storm of Greece;
Tumult tossed round me, rising with the years.
What was that Pale Boy's name the gossips set
By mine? . . . we dead so easily forget!

THE SINGLE ARROW

There were two warriors who went forth to fight:
The first with courage armed, the last with fright:
The first strode, bold, to where the battle broke,
And took, unharmed, the foeman's fiercest stroke;
The second, far from where the battle reeled,
Crouched, as he hoped, behind his saving shield.
But—victory coming at the edge of day—
It was the first who strode, unscathed, away;
While he who crouched, safe from the trampling rout,—
Fear, with her single arrow, found him out!

WAKE, MY LOVE
(A Dune Aubade)

O, wake, my Love, the day is young;
It brings a new song to be sung,—
   Wake, my Love!
The heaven about is all a-shine;
The air tastes sweet as any wine,—
   O, wake, my Love!

I wear your kiss upon my lips;
I feel keen to the finger-tips,—
   Wake, my Love!
We'll share again another day
Before the night come, old and grey,—
   O, wake, my Love!

CALENDAR OF MY DAYS

I'll write down in the calendar of my days
So many things that people do not rate:
Often the white moon going up her ways
Like a great queen in state,—
But mostly what the world calls little things,
Put to one side with unregardedness:
The momentary flash of sunbright wings;
A girl's escaping tress
Before she gathers it again; or word
Given me for heart's ease beyond my hope;
Voices of hidden birds before unheard;
A grassblade's heliotrope
Losing its green in dusk; the evening star
Putting upon the waves its lucent path,
Leading me, bright and far,
Beyond this rolling world of might and wrath,
With sweet, small, holy power!

IF THINGS WERE THINGS ONLY

There are small noises in the gloom;
The chairs have life about the room,
And undetected motions go
Under the moonlight's pale-cast glow.
O!—
What worth were philosophy
Art, Music, Sculpture, Poetry,
If things were only things we see?

HORACE ON HIS SABINE FARM

Horace, on his Sabine farm,
Enjoyed a kingdom without harm;
And his spring-born, skipping lamb
By its silly, bleating dam,—
To see it dancing, mincing, skipping,
The sun up at the morning peeping,—
Afforded him such happy fun
His laughter woke with day begun;
While his Greek Girl, soft, did creep,
Back to his bed while he feigned sleep . . .
Soon they got up, sprightly both,
She to serve him nothing loth,
With his breakfast, as in bed—
All appetites replenished.
From the bright, Bandusian brook
A jar to mix with wine she took:
Through his veins the mixture glowed,
While he wrote another ode.

HE WHO HAS HEARD

He who has heard the voices of the sea
Become articulate like human speech
And waves' revealments on the murmuring beach
Has found, already, immortality:
He fears no wrecks; each shell's an argosy
Of rich reverberance; every cove and reach
Affords him thoughts the tongue's dearth may not teach:
He breaks the threads of fate and destiny.

And never any cargo he bears forth
Except the greatness of the heart and mind.
He puts aside all gain as nothingness.
He needs no star that sits firm in the North—
No tempest full of foam and black with wind
Can bring upon his soul one feared distress!

THE SUN AND THE MOON

The sun is a flighty girl
    With gold in every curl;
But the moon's my Queen;
Look at her where she goes;
Each cloud with silver glows
    With stars between.
Upon the wave-top lies
A touch of bright surprise
    From her soft beams.
O, Moon, my lovely bride,
Couch softly by my side,
    And bring me dreams!

HUMAN, AFTER ALL

The day has gone; the night is come,
Its bosom full of stars; the foam
Wanders, pale, in dusk; the Town
Is full of lights like stars come down:
Let's get in before the bars
Close,—abandoning the stars!

IN MEMORIAM
Bossy McGady

Psalms XXIV, 1: The earth is the Lord's and the fullness thereof.
Psalms XXIII, 5: Thou preparest a table before me.

He looked on Living with a kindly sense
And held it wrong to stint on opulence;
His guest was king who hardly could do wrong:
That's why I celebrate my friend in song!
O, these poor, pallid people who protest
That to but sip at God's full gift is best,
I'll have none of them; they scant heaven's feast,
And earth's,—to say the most of them, and least!

To me this is the Deity's deepest sense,
That men should share earth's fullest opulence:
As our friend, who has gone, in living taught
And merrily in this mortal vineyard wrought.
He loved the fullness of thy earth, O Lord
With every good thing by thy bounty stored,—
Not thy mere footstool but an opulent place;
And thy world's banquet he did not disgrace
Where thou sent'st forth to call all to partake
Of wondrous viands for Love's only sake;
Where the pale waters' Urge unto their Lord
Reddened to wine, and served the marriage-board,
Where Cana's jars, miraculous, bore the test
So that the feasters found the last draughts best.

Gone is our friend, emptying half the year—
To bring up round a brighter hemisphere;
For, if we lose his day, dawn is not done:
His morning looks upon another sun.
He takes his voice and laugh to greater ends:
That man who is a friend never lacks friends!

He is a fool who thinks death hushes all
Or souls can be quenched by a funeral . . .
This was the man our friendship came to know.
If I transgress,—forgive! It still is so!